IMAGES OF WAR
ROYAL FLYING CORPS

IMAGES OF WAR
ROYAL FLYING CORPS

ALISTAIR SMITH

Pen & Sword
AVIATION

First published in Great Britain in 2012 by
P E N & S W O R D   A V I A T I O N
an imprint of
Pen & Sword Books Ltd,
47 Church Street, Barnsley,
South Yorkshire.
S70 2AS

ISBN 978-1-84884-889-4

A CIP catalogue record for this book is available
from the British Library

Typeset by Mac Style, Beverley, East Yorkshire
Printed and bound by CPI Group (UK) Ltd, Croydon, CR0 4YY

Pen & Sword Books Ltd incorporates the imprints of
Pen & Sword Books Ltd incorporates the Imprints of Pen & Sword Aviation,
Pen & Sword Family History, Pen & Sword Maritime, Pen & Sword Military, Pen & Sword
Discovery, Wharncliffe Local History, Wharncliffe True Crime, Wharncliffe Transport,
Pen & Sword Select, Pen & Sword Military Classics, Leo Cooper, The Praetorian Press,
Remember When, Seaforth Publishing and Frontline Publishing

For a complete list of Pen & Sword titles please contact:
PEN & SWORD BOOKS LIMITED
47 Church Street, Barnsley, South Yorkshire, S70 2AS, England.
E-mail: enquiries@pen-and-sword.co.uk
Website: www.pen-and-sword.co.uk

Contents

Introduction

This book focuses on the Royal Flying Corps, which came about as a result of deliberations by the Committee of Imperial Defence in 1911. The Royal Flying Corps came into existence on April 13 1912, when King George V signed the official Royal Warrant. The Committee of Imperial Defence had recommended in February 1912 that a Flying Corps should be created. Initially it would consist of four elements, which were:

- A Naval Wing
- A Military Wing
- A Central Flying School
- An aircraft factory

By the end of 1912 the Flying Corps, which came under the overall responsibility of the Director of Military Training, Brigadier-General Henderson, had a strength of 133 officers and had access to thirty six aircraft and twelve balloons.

The motto of the Royal Flying Corps, which has become the motto of the Royal Air Force, was *Per Ardua Ad Astra*, which translated means *Through Adversity to the Stars*.

Almost from the outset there were issues between the Army and the Royal Navy. Both felt that they had differing priorities. As far as the Army was concerned it would be the role of the Royal Flying Corps to undertake photographic reconnaissance and to provide spotting duties for their artillery. These were not, however, the views of the Royal Navy and they wanted to have their own aircraft. These would primarily deal with reconnaissance, spotting for the ship-borne artillery and hunting for enemy shipping whilst ensuring that Royal Navy vessels were not spotted. To begin with the Military Wing consisted of three squadrons. The Naval Wing separated itself from the Royal Flying Corps in 1914.

What was particularly remarkable about the Royal Flying Corps was its enormous growth over an incredibly short period of time. We need to bear in mind that aircraft were relatively new inventions, but that nations had already seen their potential value. Prior to the outbreak of the First World War it is unlikely that aircraft were viewed by many as an offensive wing of the armed forces. Indeed they were seen very much as a support arm.

When the Royal Flying Corps was created in 1912 the very first three squadrons were formed from the Air Battalion of the Royal Engineers. These became Squadron Nos 1, 2 and

3. Squadron No 4 was created out of the newly formed Squadron No 2 in August 1912. The fifth squadron was added out of Squadron No 3 in July 1913. At this stage there were very few pilots, but by the end of March 1918 the Royal Flying Corps could boast 150 squadrons.

The photographs featured in this book have been taken from four different photographic albums. These belonged to men who served in the Royal Flying Corps. One of the albums focuses on Tangmere, which is now the home of the Tangmere Military Aviation Museum. It is based near Chichester in West Sussex. Tangmere is, of course, well known for its role in the Battle of Britain, but it was founded in 1917. The Royal Flying Corps used it as a training base until 1918, when it became a training centre for American pilots. They continued to use it until November 1918. It was then mothballed for seven years but reopened to be used by the Fleet Air Arm in 1925. By 1939 it had been identified as a key location to protect the south coast of England against the threat of the Luftwaffe.

The second album was owned by a Royal Flying Corps serviceman who received his training in Canada. The training organisation was set up in 1917 and consisted of three stations. The stations became incredibly important in terms of training officers and other ranks. As we will see when we examine the album in detail, although there was no danger from enemy aircraft in Canada, this was not to mean that the training was not dangerous. In fact there were around 130 fatal crashes in Canada by the end of the First World War.

The third album belonged to Flight Lieutenant W Richards. This is the most extensive of all of the albums in this particular collection. It is clear that Richards also became involved with the Royal Flying Corps in around 1917. There are several photographs of his training and numerous images of crashed and wrecked aircraft.

The final album features aircraft in and around the River Crouch in Essex. This part of the country has a particular connection with military aviation. In 2009 a site known as South Fambridge celebrated its 100th anniversary of experimental flights, which took off from meadows surrounding the River Crouch. The site is claimed to be the oldest airfield in Britain, although some suggest that it is in fact Leysdown on the Isle of Sheppey. Pioneers used Fambridge in 1909 but ultimately the site itself is much less well known that Leysdown. There are two main reasons for this – the Wright brothers visited Leysdown and Fambridge was little more than a bog at the time. Nonetheless we know that there were early seaplane trials on the River Crouch at Fambridge. We know that in 1914 early flying boats made their first flights from Fambridge. This was probably as a result of the boat building tradition along the River Crouch and we also know that the *Talbot Quick* was actually built at Fambridge. This was an early prototype flying boat. The maiden flight was a disaster, however, as a mechanic was drowned and the plane had to be abandoned. Today Fambridge is pretty much forgotten as an aviation site, but a memorial was unveiled in February 2009 by the Airfields of Britain Conservation Trust. The granite block proudly recounts Fambridge's contribution to aviation history for future generations.

The photographic albums are owned by James Payne. High resolution scans of these photographic albums and many more can be found at his website, www.throughtheireyes2.co.uk.

It has not been possible to use all of the photographs from the four albums in question. It must be recognised that these are early photographs and they were not taken by a professional photographer, hence in some cases the quality of the images are variable. Since the scans were taken from prints and not from negatives some of the photographs have been subject to a bleaching effect from the sun and degrading chemicals. However, considering the age of the photographs (around 100 years old), they are remarkably sharp and provide a hitherto unseen set of images of the Royal Flying Corps in the years just before and during the First World War.

Chapter 1

Tangmere

When the First World War broke out in August 1914, only Squadron Nos 2, 3, 4 and 5 had aircraft. Squadron No 1 at this stage had balloons, but this equipment was turned over to the Royal Navy and, in time, they were equipped with their own aircraft.

The first sixty Royal Flying Corps aircraft left Dover on August 13 1914. They made for Boulogne and then towards Amiens, and ultimately to Maubeuge. Even before the Royal Flying Corps was engaged in aerial missions they had lost two of their men. A pilot, Robert R Skene, and his air mechanic were both killed when they crashed at Netheravon the day before the squadrons left Dover.

Squadron No 1, now equipped with aircraft, followed the other squadrons over to France a few days later. Officially the Royal Flying Corps undertook its first mission on August 19 1914. It was undertaken in poor weather. Two pilots, without their observers, were sent off to carry out a reconnaissance; one got lost and had to return home but the other successfully carried out his mission. Just three days later the Royal Flying Corps lost their first aircraft in combat. A newly arrived Avro 504 of Squadron No 5 was shot down by rifle fire over Belgium, killing the pilot and his observer.

On the very same day the first crucial contribution made by the Royal Flying Corps took place. A Royal Flying Corps aircraft saw the 1st German Army trying to work its way around the flank of the British Expeditionary Force. Had they not spotted this the likelihood is that the British Army would have been cut off and surrounded. In the event, the British Expeditionary Force commander, Field Marshal Sir John French, made necessary moves to block the Germans, which led to the battle of Mons.

The Royal Flying Corps was engaged directly in the battle of Mons, which began on August 23 1914. Just two days later the Royal Flying Corps claimed its first kill when an Avro 504 forced down a German Etrich Taube aircraft. Mons was a defeat for the British and the expeditionary force began falling back towards Marne. Once again it was the Royal Flying Corps that spotted the Germans trying to get around the flank of the French forces. Their observation allowed the French to counterattack just in time.

Throughout the course of the First World War the responsibilities of the Royal Flying Corps were many and varied. One of the new roles was to carry out photo reconnaissance and to use wireless telegraphy. The first really useful aerial camera did not become available until around 1915. These were semi-automatic cameras and they could be fitted to a hole in the bottom of the fuselage or strapped to the side of the fuselage. If the aircraft was flying at around 16,000ft it could take a very good shot of the landscape below, covering at least a 2sqm area.

Wireless telegraphy proved to be invaluable in assisting the fall of artillery shells. This was a second, important role carried out by Royal Flying Corps aircraft. The aircraft would be sent up and could report on where the first ranging shots or the barrage itself was landing in relation to the intended target. Using wireless telegraphy the aircraft could communicate directly with the artillery unit and help them adjust their aim. The major problem with the early telegraphy units was that they were large and heavy. The other issue was that they could only send and not receive. The consequence of this was that the pilot would have to fly, navigate, observe and send messages, converting them into Morse code, all at the same time. The artillery unit receiving the message from the aircraft was not even able to request a repeat of the message if the pilot had made an error.

Over the course of time there were improvements made and one such was the so-called Zone Call. Maps of the area were gridded and the pilot could send by Morse the precise square in which the target was located. This still needed an enormous amount of skill.

As the war progressed, by the spring of 1915, limited bombing raids were carried out by the Royal Flying Corps. The first one was against a railway station. It was not until the autumn of 1917 that any form of strategic bombing was really mounted.

One of the other key issues for the Royal Flying Corps was to help British troops on the ground when they were launching an offensive, or facing a determined attack by the Germans. This was achieved by a combination of machine guns and bomb racks. Carrying out attacks against German ground targets at incredibly low altitude required nerves of steel, as it was incredibly dangerous and ground troops quickly learned that Royal Flying Corps aircraft were vulnerable even to rifle fire. It should be noted that armoured aircraft were not available throughout the course of the First World War. Royal Flying Corps squadrons engaged in ground attack missions could expect a high attrition rate.

This album, as with two of the other albums in this book, primarily seems to focus on the training of Royal Flying Corps personnel. Photographs taken by pilots over the trenches in Europe are incredibly rare. The men that were recruited into the Royal Flying Corps came from a variety of different backgrounds. Many of the pilots were actually seconded from infantry units. Their first role was that of an observer. They were not really trained until at least 1917, hence it is significant that many of the photographs in this particular collection date around that time. Prior to formal training an observer would become fully qualified only by carrying out observation missions.

There was a peculiar relationship between the pilot and the observer. Technically the pilot was nothing more than a driver and it was the observer that was in command of the aircraft. Some of the observers could, in an emergency situation, take over control of the aircraft, but the vast majority of the aircraft in any case did not have dual control. This meant that if the pilot was killed or badly injured then the aircraft was almost certain to crash. Ultimately, the command roles were reversed, as it was recognised that it was the pilot that should command the aircraft.

Certainly in the initial stages of the First World War pilot training was fairly rudimentary. Large numbers of the trainee pilots actually died as a result of crashes, even before they had seen action. This meant that an entirely new approach had to be developed. It was decided to set up proper training centres and develop a comprehensive training programme.

By the late spring of 1916 a number of flying schools had been set up across Britain and indeed there were advanced training schools, which were run by fully qualified pilots. These men would try to replicate the kind of combat conditions that the newly trained pilots would have to face.

It should also be noted that the Royal Flying Corps was not an all-British affair. There were large numbers of Australians, New Zealanders, Canadians and South Africans. Before the United States entered the war in 1917 there were upwards of 200 American pilots serving in the Royal Flying Corps. The biggest contribution in terms of nationality was from the Canadians. A full one third of Royal Flying Corps aircrew were Canadian.

This photographic album consists predominantly of photographs of aircraft and we know that the owner of this album was certainly at Tangmere from at least 1917. Tangmere became an airfield as a result of an accident. On November 19 1916 a trainee pilot, Lieutenant Geoffrey Dorman, was in the process of completing his twenty hour solo flying in order to gain his wings. He was making a cross-country flight between Shoreham and Gosport in his FE2B, serial number 4875. He began to encounter engine problems and, in fact, his engine failed. Unfortunately there was a heavy mist and he took the decision to try to land on open ground in the country, rather than risk limping on towards Portsmouth. Luckily for Dorman the mist cleared and he managed to nurse his aircraft down into a field. When he got back to base at Gosport he told his senior officers that it was an ideal location for an airfield. Whether it was as a consequence of this recommendation or not, the government bought 200 acres in the following year, which would become Tangmere. It was in use from September 1917, primarily for flight training.

Of course we know that Tangmere was an incredibly important and famous base during the Second World War. It became an operational station for the RAF in 1926 and the first two Tangmere squadrons were numbers 1 and 43. In 1939 Tangmere became sector headquarters for No 11 Group Fighter Command. It was to play a crucial role in the defence of southern England and London over the course of the war. The station grew considerably and there were extensions to the runway carried out in 1941. RAF Signals Command took over the airfield in 1958. The station was finally closed in 1970. To signify the long association with the Royal Flying Corps and the RAF a solitary Spitfire's growling engine merged with the plaintive sound of the last post on October 16 1970.

This is a Sopwith Camel, which has force landed in what appears to be a sugar beet field near to Tangmere. Note that the wings have already been removed and that there are signs that the aircraft dipped as it came in to land and that one of the propeller blades has virtually been sheared off. The Sopwith Camel was a direct replacement for the Sopwith Pup. The first prototype was flown on December 22 1916. This aircraft has already had its twin Vickers machine guns removed, or, perhaps, if it was a training aircraft, it may not have had the machine guns fitted. Just less than 5,500 of these aircraft were built. The Sopwith Camel was a tremendous aircraft, with heavy armament, light controls and superb manoeuvrability. It went into service with Squadron No 4 in June 1917. By the spring of 1918 thirteen squadrons also had the Sopwith Camel. The most famous pilot was Major William Barker, who flew B6313. From September 1917 to September 1918 he flew just over 400 operational hours. During this time he shot down forty six German balloons and aircraft. This made the B6313 the most successful individual aircraft ever flown, either by the Royal Flying Corps or the RAF.

These are two Royal Flying Corps trainee officers. It has been possible to trace the individual on the right of the photograph as Second-Lieutenant Leonard Randles. The other individual is captioned on the photograph as being Lieutenant Hood. Unfortunately little can be discovered about the fortunes of either of these two men. Randles is wearing an official Royal Flying Corps uniform but the man on the left, Hood, looks to be wearing his original regimental uniform. Randles' uniform is what was commonly known as the 'maternity smock'. It is cut rather like an infantry jacket but has a distinctive fly front. On his shoulders would have been a white on dark navy blue Royal Flying Corps emblem, but in this photograph they do not appear to be present. He is wearing a side cap.

This is a second photograph of the two men featured in the previous shot. Again they are in a relaxed pose. Once the men had been transferred to combat duties in France they were driven very hard and newcomers would have comparatively little flying time or combat experience. In April 1916 the Royal Flying Corps was losing thirty per cent of its aircraft and aircrew each week. In that month alone they lost 151 aircraft and 316 aircrew. The life expectancy of pilots and crew on the Western Front during this period of time was twenty three days. No small wonder that April 1916 was dubbed 'Bloody April'.

This photograph is captioned 'Lieutenant Hood and self crashed mid-air with Camel at Tangmere February 12'. This is not a Camel, but is in fact an Avro 504k trainer. It was manufactured, as can be seen on the fuselage, by Sage of Peterborough. Sage began as a shop fitting company. The business was established in Hatton Garden in 1860 by Frederick Sage. When Sage died in 1898 the business was run by three of his nephews, who became partners along with Sage's son. They were to experience great highs before the First World War, fitting out Harrods in Knightsbridge, D H Evans in Oxford Street, Selfridges and providing the interiors for many of the huge P&O and Cunard liners. In 1915 they were contracted to become an aircraft manufacturer. They used their Peterborough factory to make cabins for airships and then went on to build more than 400 Avro 504s and received a contract to built over 100 Sopwith Camels, but this was cancelled when the war ended in 1918. Sage even began developing their own aircraft alongside the aircraft designer Eric Cecil Gordon England. They tried to develop the Sage Types I-IV but it was largely a failure and the aircraft manufacturing part of the business closed down in 1918. They were involved in aircraft manufacture again in the Second World War, making fuselages for Horsa gliders and there were plans for them to build wings for naval aircraft. The business had run into trouble by the 1960s and became a subsidiary of British Electric Traction, later BET and subsequently was purchased by Rentokil in 1968.

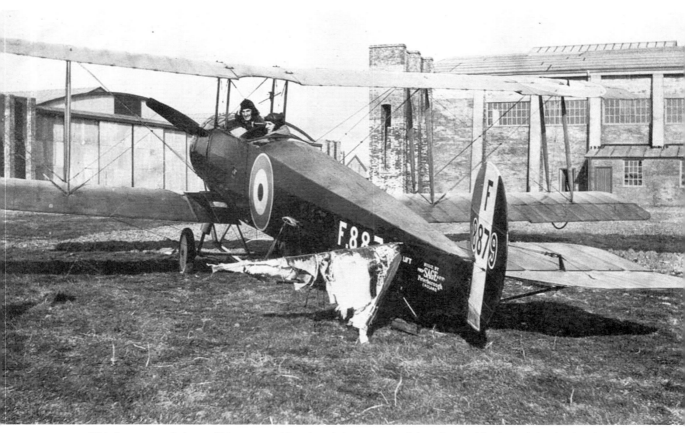

This is a second shot of Lieutenant Hood and the owner of the album, this time sitting in the Avro 504 trainer that had been involved in the collision with the Sopwith Camel.

This photograph is captioned as showing Lieutenants Dixon, Dalton and Wright at Tangmere. It is particularly interesting to note the three distinctively different types of uniform being worn by the men. Dixon is wearing what appears to be his original army uniform, with Royal Flying Corps badges. Dalton is wearing the RFC maternity style jacket, whilst Wright is also wearing his original British Army uniform but he also has a Royal Flying Corps peaked cap and he is wearing puttees.

A Bristol M1C is featured in this photograph. It bears the aircraft serial number C4940. This was a monoplane that made its maiden flight in July 1916. A handful of these aircraft were used in the Middle East and in the Balkans, but the vast majority were used by British-based training units. Around 130 of the aircraft were built.

The serial number on this aircraft appears to be H2742 and it is a Sopwith Camel. In all likelihood this was attached to the training unit. One of the other key roles for the Sopwith Camel was for home defence and it was this aircraft that was used by the Royal Naval Air Service operating out of Manston and Eastchurch and deployed to cope with German Gotha bomber raids from July 1917. By August 1918 seven home defence squadrons were using the aircraft.

This is another Sopwith Camel, this time bearing the serial number F3115. The serial block F3096-F3145 was all allocated to Sopwith Camels. Some of the aircraft were actually converted to become two-seaters for training purposes. The Sopwith Camel usually had a crew of just one. It had a wingspan of 8.53m and was 5.71m long. It had a maximum speed of 115mph, a range of around 300miles and could climb at 5.5m per second. This aircraft does not appear to be armed, but it would usually have a pair of 0.303 Vickers machine guns.

This is a second photograph of the Sopwith Camel sitting in the sugar beet field. This aircraft is obviously going nowhere, as it has a broken propeller.

Although partially obscured, the serial number of this Bristol F2B appears to begin F476, which was part of a number of aircraft running from F4271 through to F4970. Over 5,300 of these aircraft were built. The first aircraft flew on September 9 1916. It was a formidable machine and perfectly capable of handling itself against all German single-seat aircraft. Unfortunately the first Bristol F2As that went on patrol in April 1917 ran into von Richthofen's squadron, consisting of Albatross D111s. Out of the six British aircraft four were shot down, and a fifth was badly shot up.

Recovering a partially wrecked Sopwith Camel from a sugar beet field somewhere in England can be seen here. The repair crew has arrived and has begun dismantling the aircraft so that it can be moved from the sugar beet field. Although the angle has not been kind to us, it would appear that the men have arrived in a Crossley light tender. The Crossley motor factory was able to churn out around forty five of these each week. Around 6,000 were built by the time the Germans surrendered in 1918. The first of the vehicles had been supplied to the Royal Flying Corps in 1913 and they had fifty six of them on the books. Theoretically, by the time the Royal Flying Corps squadrons were fully operational they were supposed to have nine tenders and one staff touring car version. It was highly unlikely that any of the squadrons ever had the full amount that was supposed to have been allocated to them. The vehicles were highly adaptable and, in this instance, it is being used as a mobile workshop.

Although it is difficult to make out this incredibly rare photograph, it is likely that this is a German Gotha GV bomber serial number 936/16, which was forced down by Captain George Hackwill. He was on home defence operations with No 44 Squadron on January 28 1918. He was awarded the Military Cross for his gallantry. Hackwill was very persistent in his hunting of this aircraft. The engagement lasted a considerable time and he was under constant fire from the enemy aircraft. The victory was shared with Lieutenant Charles C Banks, who was also awarded the Military Cross for his involvement in the action.

These are Avro 504s. Production of these aircraft began in 1913 and did not cease until 1932. By this stage 10,000 of them had been built, with just less than 9,000 being produced during the First World War alone. It was a development of the Avro 500, which had been designed primarily for private flying and for training.

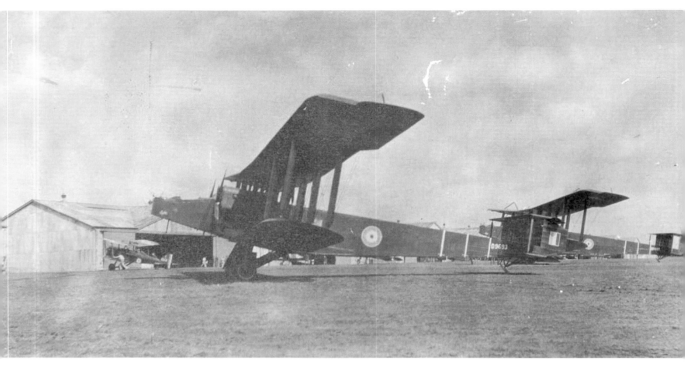

The serial number on this aircraft is D9693, which was part of a range of serials allocated to Handley Page 0/400 aircraft. When it was constructed it was the largest aircraft that had ever been built by the British. The 0/400 had a crew of four or five and could carry over 900kg of bombs, as well as five Lewis guns to protect it. This was a later version of the 0/100 and was introduced in 1918, with some 400 being allocated to squadrons before the armistice.

Although the quality of this photograph is relatively poor, we can see more clearly the tail section of the aircraft. Whilst on first impression the markings might suggest a French aircraft, this is in fact the standard markings for British aircraft. Had the photograph been slightly clearer it might have been possible to read the serial number, which was written across the red, white and blue on the tail. It is possible only to make out what appears to be 96, which does not narrow down the identity of the aircraft at all. What is possible to see is that the aircraft does have two cockpits, which shows that it is a trainer version of the Sopwith Camel.

This is a second photograph of the same aircraft. We can see that it is standing on grass outside a hangar, with a similar aircraft to the rear.

Three of the four men in this shot are wearing the classic Royal Flying Corps leather flying jackets. These were mid-tan with asymmetrical fronts. They had an angled map pocket to the side and were belted at the waist, with flapped pockets on each side. Given the fact that the cockpits were open, leather coats such as this were a real bonus. The men wore several layers of underwear and their uniform tunic underneath the coat. If they could find them, they would also wear leather trousers and overshoes. The problem was that the uniform tunic had to be worn in order to comply with the Geneva Convention. The danger was that they would be accused of being spies if they did not have a clear uniform. We can also see that the men are wearing leather helmets, triplex goggles and fur-lined gauntlets. They are also wearing silk scarves around their necks to prevent chaffing.

These Royal Flying Corps men have settled down outside their tent in an unnamed field. The man on the left of the photograph is holding a British standard issue Lee Enfield 303 rifle. These were first produced in 1907. A trained man could fire off twelve shots in a minute. On the Western Front the men found that unless they kept their rifles spotlessly clean the Lee Enfield was susceptible to dirt and mud. Many of them wrapped cloth around the firing mechanism. The cleaning equipment was kept in the butt of the rifle.

This is a slightly faded photograph of some of the officers and aircrew horsing around with a Lewis gun. This weapon was invented by Colonel Isaac Newton Lewis, a US Army colonel, in 1911. The Americans did not actually take it up so Lewis moved to Belgium and then Britain. Eventually the Birmingham Small Arms Company began manufacturing the weapon in 1914. Note the distinctive PAN magazine. There were in fact two different sorts of drum magazine; one could hold forty seven rounds and the other ninety seven. The British bought tens of thousands of these and in fact over 50,000 had been made in Britain and the United States by the end of the First World War. The cost of the Lewis gun in 1915 was £165.00.

This is a German Albatross that was captured after an action involving the Royal Naval Air Service over Dunkirk. Two Albatross aircraft, which survive today, were in fact captured. One is in the National Air and Space Museum in Washington DC. This one was captured in the spring of 1918. On December 17 1917 a second aircraft had landed behind Commonwealth lines and the aircraft was recovered with the pilot being captured. As the pilot and aircraft had been captured by Australian troops this one was handed over to the Australian Flying Corps. It is now on view at the Australian War Memorial, Anzac Hall in Canberra.

The serial number of this aircraft is E6184. This is a Sopwith Snipe, according to the serial number. The Snipe was a relative latecomer to the First World War, as designs did not begin until the spring of 1917. The first prototype was ready by the autumn. The Royal Flying Corps put in an order for 1,700 in March 1918. In all some 4,500 were ordered, including those destined for other air forces. Production actually ended in 1919, by which time just 500 had been built. The Snipe did see action with No 43 Squadron from late August 1918 and with the Australian Flying Corps' No 4 Squadron from October 1918.

This is a second photograph of the Sopwith Snipe, E6184. The Snipe with serial number E8102 was being flown by a Canadian, Major William G Barker, on October 27 1918. He was attached to RAF Squadron No 201 and carrying out an evaluation flight over France. Barker engaged a German aircraft and shot it down. He was then set upon by no fewer than fifteen Fokker DVIIs. In the desperate struggle Barker, who eventually had to make a forced landing, was wounded on three occasions. He apparently lost consciousness at least once but managed to shoot down three of the German aircraft. For his gallantry he was awarded the Victoria Cross. Luckily part of this aircraft, the fuselage, is actually in the Canadian War Museum in Ottawa.

The Snipes that were assigned to the Australian Flying Corps' No 4 Squadron saw considerable action in the last few days of October 1918. In the period October 26 to 29 the unit lost fifteen Snipes. In return, on the 26th they shot down five German aircraft, six on October 28, and eight on October 29 and, in addition to this on the same day, they forced two more German aircraft to crash land.

This rather bleached photograph shows a Sopwith Camel that has seriously come to grief. Note the damage to the upper wings which appear to have sheared off on impact with the ground. The serial number appears to be B7177. This means that the photograph would have been taken probably in 1918. By this time 13 RFC and RNAS squadrons had been equipped with the aircraft. Later, this would rise to 50 squadrons. Despite its relatively short service period in what remained of the First World War, pilots flying the Sopwith Camel shot down nearly 1300 enemy aircraft.

This is a shot of an Avro 504 trainer. Both the Royal Flying Corps and the Royal Naval Air Service had begun purchasing limited numbers of this aircraft before the outbreak of the First World War. The Avro 504 has an unfortunate reputation in as much as it was the first Royal Flying Corps aircraft to be shot down by the Germans. This took place on August 22 1914. It was being piloted by Second-Lieutenant Vincent Waterfall and the navigator was Lieutenant Charles Bayly. They belonged to No 5 Squadron.

It would appear that this photograph is a SIA7B. It was designed by the Fiat Company and entered service with the Italian air force in November 1917. Unfortunately its wings were not very durable and the pilot had a poor view. What is interesting is that this photograph appears to have been taken possibly at Martlesham Heath or Cranwell, where it was being evaluated at the Aeroplane Experimental Station.

This is a second photograph of the SIA7B. It was originally designed to be a reconnaissance aircraft and it was meant to replace some of the earlier reconnaissance aircraft being used. It is quite possible that this photograph was taken in September 1917. Captain Giulio Laureati flew from Turin to Naples and then returned, covering 1,000miles in ten and a half hours. He undertook this flight on August 15 1917. He then flew on September 24 from Turin to London, covering the distance in six hours. It is perfectly possible that these photographs were taken to commemorate this flight.

This final shot in the set of three may well show Marquis Giulio Laureati, although unfortunately this cannot be confirmed. He was born in 1877 and died in 1943. At the age of twenty he was conscripted into an Italian engineering unit and by 1912 he had acquired his pilot's licence. During the First World War he flew over 1,600 hours. At various times he worked for the technical director of army aviation in Turin. He was also involved in operations against the enemy. When he arrived in Britain in September 1917 he was actually received by King George V and awarded the Royal Victorian Order.

It is believed that these are Armstrong Whitworth FK3s. These were primarily used by the Royal Flying Corps and around 500 of them were built. The aircraft was designed by a Dutchman, hence the FK in the title of the aircraft, standing for Frederick Koolhoven. The Royal Flying Corps used it as a general purpose aircraft and as a trainer. Operationally it had a single Lewis gun mounted to the rear of the cockpit, as can be seen in this photograph, and, as an alternative, if flown as a single-seater aircraft; it could carry just over 50kg of bombs. The aircraft had a wing span of 12.19m, the overall length of the aircraft was 8.84m, and it had a maximum speed at sea level of 89mph and could operate at altitudes up to 3,660m.

Chapter 2

The Royal Flying Corps in Canada

Unfortunately it is unclear whether the original owner of this album was British or Canadian. The photographs chronicle Royal Flying Corps training and aircraft mishaps in Canada.

Canada was recognised as being a potentially fertile area to attract recruits for both the Royal Flying Corps and the Royal Naval Air Service. At the beginning of the First World War all that was required of a potential recruit was that they had a valid pilot's licence. Many men wanted to take the opportunity of joining either of the services. The simple fact was that the existing training school infrastructure in Canada could not cope with the demand. In any case, the men were expected to pay for their own pilot training. At the same time both the Royal Flying Corps and the Royal Naval Air Service, which were growing at a tremendous rate, discovered that there was insufficient flight training opportunities in Britain as well.

It was decided in 1917 to set up a comprehensive flight training programme in Canada. The plans were very ambitious; there would be four training schools that would each be allocated at least one or more airfields and up to five squadrons would be trained at each school at any given time. In the event there were some amendments, which pared the plan down to three training schools.

Camp Borden in Ontario was chosen as the primary site. There would also be a station at Desoronto, also in Ontario and another at North Toronto. Five training squadrons and an aerial gunnery school were opened at Camp Borden, five more at Desoronto and three at North Toronto.

As early as September 1914 Canada had begun preparations to create their own Canadian Aviation Corps. It had very modest beginnings and many potential Canadian pilots went straight into the Royal Flying Corps or the Royal Naval Air Service rather than the Canadian force. In fact Canada did not have its own national air service during the First World War, but many of the very best Royal Flying Corps pilots were in fact Canadian.

When the United States became an ally in April 1917 the immediate advantage was a new influx of potential pilots. Many Americans were shipped to Canada to carry out training. Ultimately, Fort Worth in Texas was chosen as an American training base and this meant that much of the training that was being carried out at Borden and Desoronto ceased.

It is interesting to speculate exactly when this clutch of photographs was taken, as there was a relatively short window during which significant amounts of training were carried out in Canada. Hence we can probably date these photographs as having been taken at some point between May and November 1917. There was still training going on at North Toronto, but this was radically reduced during this time.

The other alternative is that these photographs were actually taken in 1918. It was decided, in April 1918, to re-establish the training stations in Canada and also to set up advanced flight training schools. When Germany surrendered on November 11 1918 there was just short of 12,000 Royal Flying Corps (now Royal Air Force) personnel in Canada. Of these just less than 5,000 were undergoing flight training.

The Royal Flying Corps and later the RAF were involved in Canada for some twenty one months. Over 3,000 pilots had successfully negotiated the training programmes and over 2,500 of these had been shipped to Europe.

It is perfectly possible that the owner of this album was in fact Canadian. He would have been one of over 23,000 Canadians that served either in the Royal Flying Corps or the Royal Naval Air Service. As mentioned many of these Canadians paid for their own training. It is worth mentioning two notable individuals.

It is generally recognised that Arthur Ince was the first Canadian to shoot down an enemy aircraft. This took place just off the coast of Belgium on December 14 1915. Another pilot was John Bernard Brophy, generally known as Don. He had made for Britain in December 1915. Don fought on the Western Front and was unfortunately killed when his aircraft began to break up on Christmas Eve 1916.

The Canadians' experiences in the Royal Air Force led directly to the creation of the Canadian Air Force. By the spring of 1918 there were some 13,000 Canadians in the RAF. By August 1918 the British Air Ministry agreed to create some Canadian only squadrons. Interestingly though, the Canadian government did not take the decision to retain an air force during peace time and one by one each of the squadrons was disbanded. The newly formed Canadian Air Force officially ceased to exist at the beginning of August 1920.

As we will see in this set of photographs, aircraft mishaps and, consequently, pilot deaths and injuries were commonplace. When Camp Borden began operations in April 1917 there were fifteen aircraft hangars, a hospital, quarters, repair shops, stores and messes. These were all temporary buildings. In the short period to September 1917 thirty two aircraft had been destroyed by the training pilots. Collectively, across Canada, seventy one aircraft had been wrecked. In fact it was at Borden that there was the first fatal accident, which occurred as early as April 8 1917, when Cadet J H Talbot died.

These individuals are relaxing on what appears to be the deck of a vessel. They are sergeants. We can see a propeller badge above the three chevrons on the left arm of the man in the foreground. The men are wearing the Royal Flying Corps maternity style jacket and have the standard type Royal Flying Corps shoulder title. When the British War Office formally announced the establishment of the Royal Flying Corps they were looking for men aged between eighteen and thirty, at least 5ft 2in and men that could serve for four years, and then a further four in reserve as a minimum. It did not matter how long the men had been in another branch of the armed services. The four years would start from the time that they were transferred into the Royal Flying Corps. Each man was on a six month probation period. The majority of the men could transfer and retain their original ranks.

This photograph shows one of the sergeants posing for the camera. It is difficult to say whether these men were fully trained flight sergeants or not. Generally a flight sergeant would have a crown embroidered onto the uniform, above the propeller, although this was by no means a universal rule. A sergeant could also be a clerk or a mechanic. The equivalent rank in the Royal Naval Air Service was a petty officer. Joining the Royal Flying Corps offered huge opportunities and was very attractive to men who felt that their careers had stalled in other services. It was relatively easy to attain the rank of warrant officer in the Royal Flying Corps and many sergeants were promoted directly into that rank. The same could be said for sergeant and first-class air mechanics, who were being recruited from existing corporals and second or third-class air mechanics. The men in the group travelling to Canada knew that their promotion prospects would be significantly improved if they learned how to fly.

These two men are corporals. When the Royal Air Force was established in April 1918 there were also corporal mechanics and clerks. Prior to that, the equivalent rank in the Royal Naval Air Service was either leading mechanic or leading aircraftman. Note that these men have two chevrons only, and they have their Royal Flying Corps shoulder badges.

This is an unidentified aircraft. It is listed as being a Sopwith Camel according to the serial number C120. Judging by the shape of the aircraft, however, it is more likely to be Curtiss JN4 Canadian. It was constructed by Canadian Aeroplanes Limited of Toronto. In the post-war period this aircraft was used by a private air service based in Montreal.

This is a second photograph of an Curtiss JN4 in Canada. Despite the numbers of these aircraft the preferred trainer was the Avro 504k. These aircraft were originally designed in 1913 and in 1918 Canada actually ordered 504 of them. When the war ended in 1918 the order was cancelled but Canada was given sixty two Avro 504s as part of a package of 114 aircraft from Britain. The rest of the Avro 504s used by the Canadians were built by the Canadian Aeroplanes Company. According to post-war records, in the period February 18 to October 18 1921 no less than ten Avro 504s were written off at Camp Borden alone. Avro 504 casualties continued into the 1920s, with the last recorded accident occurring at Winnipeg on August 13 1927.

A Royal Flying Corps sergeant poses with his swagger stick for the camera here. The Royal Canadian Air Force celebrated its seventy fifth anniversary at Borden in 1999. One of the things that the Canadians did to the Avro 504 to try and preserve the lives of men such as this was to fit skids to the front of the aircraft. This was done in order to try to prevent nose tipping when the aircraft landed. At the Toronto training school initially training took place using the Curtiss JN4 but, because this was a fairly basic aircraft, men would have to be retrained when they arrived in Britain. This led to an order of 500 Avro 504Ks to replace the Curtiss aircraft in Canada. One of the major problems was the winter months in Canada and in late 1917 it was decided not to risk the open cockpit biplanes and instead they were shipped down to Fort Worth in Texas to continue the training.

A Royal Flying Corps corporal is with an unidentified other Royal Flying Corps serviceman and two female civilians in this photograph. Being a member of the Royal Flying Corps had significant financial advantages over the regular army. Normally once a man was transferred into the Army Reserves he would receive an annual gratuity of £10. If he was placed on the First Reserve with the Royal Flying Corps as a flyer then, as long as he successfully carried out a quarterly flying test, he would receive an extra £10 per year.

Three Royal Flying Corps servicemen are seen here. The man in the centre is a corporal and the man on the right is a sergeant. When the men were enlisted they received a free outfit of clothing and all necessary equipment was supplied. They were also issued with extra clothing on a quarterly basis and given a kit allowance. The daily rates of pay for a warrant officer was 9s 0d, for a sergeant it was 6s 0d and a first class air mechanic received 4s 0d. Those that were selected to fly aircraft received an extra 1s 0d per day whilst they were at training school. Once qualified, according to their flying proficiency, they would receive either 2s 0d or 4s 0d extra per day. Men that were in receipt of flying pay were tested on a half-yearly basis. They would be reclassified as either first or second class flyers.

A Royal Flying Corps sergeant is sitting on a bench by the sea in this shot. Men that were married were allocated a separation allowance, which was paid directly to their wives and families. In the event of the death of a man whilst in service then pensions and compassionate allowances were awarded to the widow and children. In addition to their regular pay men were given a messing allowance, a quarters or lodging allowance, and extra funds for fuel and light, along with rations of bread and meat.

Enjoying a pleasure cruise, possibly to visit the Niagara Falls is the focus of this photograph. Niagara Falls is relatively close to the main flight training schools that were run by the Royal Flying Corps. The cost of training these men was estimated at just under $US10,000. Organising all of the men was an extremely onerous task, as there was a continual movement of men in and out of the training squadrons. At any one time at least half of the men were either about to leave or had just arrived. This gave logistical nightmares to the quartermasters and a host of other individuals, not to mention the problems of the constant replacement of damaged or destroyed aircraft.

A sergeant is enjoying a drink from a fountain in a Canadian suburb in this photograph. A cadet would join the Cadet Wing and pass through the Recruits Depot. Here he would be given basic infantry training, as well as being shown how to use telegraphic equipment. He would also be given basic lectures on discipline and hygiene. This took around two weeks. He would remain in the Cadet Wing for eight weeks and would be given additional instruction, including aerial navigation. He would then be sent onto the School of Aeronautics and would have to absorb the basic principles of design and operation of aircraft engines.

Relaxing on Lake Niagara. After the school of aeronautics the cadet would go onto the armaments school. It was only after this that he would begin flying tuition; something no doubt he had been waiting for every since he enlisted. They were also required to practice aerial photography, bomb dropping and signalling. They would have to learn to fly in formation and to carry out cross-country flights. Usually the first flight would require the cadet to climb to around 6,000ft and to try to stay at this height for around fifteen minutes. Throughout all of this, training in physical education also played an important role. The cadets would also go to the school of aerial fighting to practice on Vickers and Lewis guns. Full size silhouettes of targets were set up on Lake Ontario for this purpose.

A corporal is posing on a pleasure steamer in this photograph. When the men came out of the training schools in Canada they were virtually ready for front line combat. Major changes came in during 1918; this was as a result of new techniques developed by Major R R Smith-Barry. It was known as the Gosport System. As opposed to the traditional way of training, which was largely theoretical, the new system was somewhat more practical. The cadets were actually shown how to put their aircraft into a spin and then how to get out of the spin.

This photograph is believed to be East Block, or Departmental Building, which is one of three buildings on Parliament Hill in Ottawa, Ontario. Construction began in 1859 and it was completed seven years later. The block is Victorian High Gothic and was designed by Thomas Stent and Augustus Laver. A new wing was added to the rear of the East Block in 1910. It was used by the last Governor General of Canada, the Earl of Athlone, who was in fact Alexander Augustus Frederick William Alfred George Cambridge (1874-1957).

Sadly the venue for this relaxed group photograph has not been captioned in the album, although it is obvious to see that the shot was taken during the spring or summer months. The individual responsible for the training organisation in Canada at the beginning was Lieutenant Colonel C G Hoare. It was primarily down to his energy and enthusiasm that by the end of the First World War there was an Armament School at Hamilton, recruiting depots and the School of Military Aeronautics at Toronto, cadet ground training at Long Branch, pilot training and the School of Special Flying at Armour Heights, the School of Aerial Fighting at Beamsville, more pilot training and the Artillery Cooperation School at Leaside and pilot training at Camps Borden, Rathbun and Mohawk.

Members of the Royal Flying Corps are seen here amongst the crowd at a Canadian military football match. Games between military sides, or military teams and civilian teams, were popular both in Britain and in Canada. In fact in Paris in 1919 there was a huge inter-allied Olympic Games style competition. In Canada football had been played since around 1876 and the Canadian Football Association was founded in 1912. Just prior to the outbreak of the First World War Norwood Wanderers became Canada's first national champions and were awarded the Connaught Cup, which had been donated by the Duke of Connaught, who at that time was Canada's governor general.

Any chance of recognising these shattered remains of this aircraft is slim, but the black cat on the fuselage actually betrays its true origin. It is an American designed and Canadian modified Curtiss JN4. Some of the aircraft were named after Canadian cities; others were named after battles from the War of 1812. This particular aircraft has a black cat, whilst others had maple leaves, shamrocks, terriers or even the Jolly Roger.

If nothing else, this second photograph of the crashed plane shows the penetrative ability and the precise aim of the pilot, who has managed to plough the Curtiss straight through the roof at virtually 90 degrees. Including American pilots, some 95 per cent of all North American pilot trainees would have flown a Curtiss JN4. Although this crash may not prove the fact, it was robust. The Canadians used the JN4 (Canadian or Canuck). These were Canadian built and in all there were around 1,260 of them. The US Air Force did actually use some of these but they discovered that due to the lighter structure of this version there were more accidents. There is an almost identical JN4 in the Canadian Aviation and Space Museum. It has the black cat insignia on the fuselage and has the registration number C227. This one was manufactured in 1918 and was bought by the museum in 1962 where it underwent significant restoration for three years from 1964. This particular aircraft was one that was used by the US Air Service and then sold off just after the First World War. Incredibly, it was put in a barn in 1932 and only came out again thirty years later when the museum bought it.

Another two Curtiss JN4 aircraft are featured in this shot. They have also come to grief, this time by colliding into one another. Note the serpent insignia on the right-hand aircraft. Perhaps the most famous flyer of a Curtiss JN4 Canuck was Amelia Eyrhart, who was born in 1897 and disappeared, presumed dead, in 1937. She had been bitten by the flying bug after her father paid for a ten minute flight for her on December 28 1920. Somehow she managed to save $1,000 by working around the clock on various job.s She made her way to an airfield near Long Beach to be taught by Anita Snook Southern, who was a pioneer aviator and the first woman to run her own aviation business and commercial airfield. Amelia Eyrhart learnt how to fly in a Curtiss JN4.

Two more crashed aircraft which appear to have collided after the leading aircraft's fixed wheel assembly has collapsed and the second one has ploughed into it. This must be on the same field as the previous photograph, as the buildings in the background appear to be the same. According to the serial numbers these are Avro 504s. They have serial numbers C703 and C753. The Canadian Aviation and Space Museum has one of these Avro 504ks also, which they acquired from a private American collector in 1968. In the post-war years the Avro 504k was the standard trainer for Canadian pilots. They were finally disposed of in 1928. Note that both the planes in this photograph bear the black cat insignia. The black cat insignia is associated with No 85 Training Squadron. This was based at Leaside Camp and part of 43 Wing. The Avro 504 was the basic trainer. A considerable number of them were sent over to Canada. They were primarily used at Camp Borden. In the period between 1920 and 1934 the Canadian Air Force, which had been re-established towards the end of 1920, operated 155 Avro 504s.

From the engine arrangement this aircraft appears to be another Curtiss JN4. It was a two-seater aircraft and at the time it was one of the most popular aircraft. It was the first mass produced North American aircraft, but it never saw action. In the post-war period literally thousands of them were sold off to civilians across America and they were seen at numerous air shows across the United States. Note the fleurs-de-lys insignia on the side of this aircraft. Portions of Canada were, of course, owned by the French until the British ejected them. Nonetheless there remained a considerable number of French speakers in Canada. At the beginning of the First World War there was considerable criticism of the French speakers, who had not been as willing to volunteer for military service as the majority of Canadians. Part of the problem was that the entire military code, being British, was in English. They preferred to try to enrol in French formations. On the Canadian National Vimy Memorial, on Hill 145, which was stormed by four Canadian divisions on April 9 1917, there is a Canadian maple leaf and a fleurs-de-lys. It serves to remember the 66,000 Canadians killed during the First World War. The fleurs-de-lys insignia is most closely associated with No 81 Training Squadron, which was based at Desoronto and part of 42 Wing.

This aircraft appears to have come to grief on a railway line. It has a serpent insignia on the fuselage and is almost unrecognisable. Fortunately we can read the aircraft's serial number in the following photograph, which identifies it as an Avro 504k. The vast majority of Avro 504ks were manufactured under license by mainly British-based factories, although Canadian Aeroplanes Limited in Toronto did build a number of these aircraft. Clearly this would have been considerably more convenient. The Avro 504k was of course a product of the Avro Aircraft Company. This had been set up by Alliott Verdon Roe in Manchester. It was the Avro 504 that kept the factory busy throughout the course of the First World War. They began to run into serious economic difficulties in the post-war period.

Another shot of the wrecked Avro 504k. To the pilot's credit at least he has managed to land between the two ditches and on the embankment of the railway. He has also managed to avoid the telegraph poles in the background. Judging by the damage on the left wing, he has in fact struck another object and this may have caused the original crash.

This is a clearer shot of the Avro 504k after it has belly-flopped onto a railway line. The fortunes of the Avro Company began to wane under the control of its original owner and in 1920 Crossley Motors acquired most of the shares and wanted the factory space to make more vehicles. Avro moved and just eight years later the business was sold to Armstrong Sidley. Roe resigned and formed another company. Avro, of course, did go on to do great things; it would be this company that would create the Manchester, Lancaster, Lincoln, Shackleton and other iconic aircraft such as the Vulcan. Unbelievably, there is still one Avro 504 that can actually fly, although it is a reproduction and is owned by a museum at the Old Rhinebeck Aerodrome in the United States. In 1971 Blue Swallow Aircraft, based in Virginia, also began making reproduction Avro 504s.

This is a Curtiss JN4, serial number C694, which has overturned. Although the damage is fairly significant, it does give us the opportunity to see the overall construction of the aircraft. Essentially it is a wooden frame with a canvas body. We can also see many of the control wires, which controlled the movement of the rudder.

It is only possible to see the last two digits of this aircraft's serial number on the tail wing. The black cat insignia indicates that the aircraft belonged to No 85 Training Squadron from Leaside. The Royal Flying Corps designated some twenty Canadian Reserve Squadrons, numbering 78 to 97. 79 Squadron began flying from Camp Borden in March 1917. By the beginning of April they had been joined by Squadron Nos 78 to 82. In the May 83, 84, 86 and 87 were at Camp Mohawk and Long Branch had 88, 89, 90 and 91. There were changes in October 1917; 42 Wing at Borden now consisted of 78, 79, 81 and 82 and in addition the School of Aerial Gunnery. 43 Wing at Desoronto had 80, 83, 84, 85, 86 and 87 and in Toronto was 44 Wing with 88, 89, 90, 91 and 92. By this stage (as of June 1917) the training squadrons, which had been known as (Canadian) Reserve Squadrons were now known as Canadian Training Squadrons.

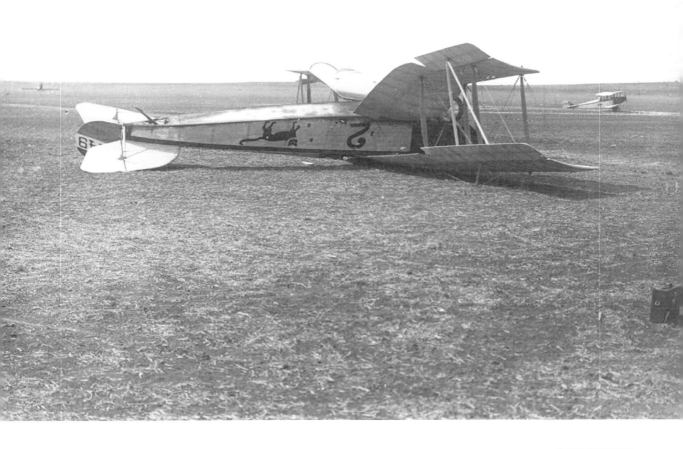

This is aircraft C446 after it has crash landed. Interestingly, the aircraft had spent the winter of 1917 to 1918 in Texas. It was then transferred to the US Air Force in July 1918, but it retained its Royal Flying Corps serial number. Somehow it must have survived, because it was sold back to Curtiss in the post-war period. Judging by the photograph, the aircraft does not seem to have been too badly damaged. Although these were flimsy machines, to some extent they were relatively easy to repair. Any broken wooden parts of the fuselage would have been far easier to replace than any damage done to the engine.

Chapter 3

Lieutenant W Richards

This album belonged to a Royal Flying Corps lieutenant by the name of Richards, possibly William. It would appear that he underwent either observer or pilot training from the spring to the summer of 1917. Some of the photographs seem to indicate that he was variously at Weybridge, Staines, Croydon and, for a brief period, in Londonderry and Belfast. The collection of photographs indicate the kind of training experience that many potential observers and pilots experienced, having been transferred from other branches of the armed services.

Initially, in order to get into the Royal Flying Corps, it was actually quite a difficult task. An officer would need a pilot's licence, or Federation Aeronautique Internationale (FAI). As the demand for pilots increased, and indeed casualties mounted, the requirement to have one of these FAI certificates had dropped away by the summer of 1916. It would seem that Richards fell into the category of typical recruits joining the Royal Flying Corps that had begun from the summer of 1916 and continued into 1917.

The Royal Flying Corps, as the youngest of all of the armed services, was reduced to making appeals to other branches of the armed services, mainly the British Army. This was an appeal to find useful candidates. Some of the men genuinely wanted to get out of regimental life, seeing the Royal Flying Corps as something of a challenge. For some it was an escape of a different guise, where they had simply not fitted into their regiment. Some candidates were not that keen and in fact many of their colleagues would tell them that they were joining a suicide club. Even men who had just come out of convalescence for fairly serious wounds were judged fit for the Royal Flying Corps, such was the cursory nature of medical examination. Some men who had chest problems were actually told that being in dry, cold air would cure them.

New recruits were told to report to various depots around the British Isles. They would first attend a ground school; one was based in Oxford and the other in Reading. Over the space of around four weeks, information would be crammed into the cadets. They were also required to do parades alongside practical programmes on wireless telegraphy or observation. They were told how to strip down a Lewis gun but there was very little taught about the mechanics of flying.

The daily routine was fairly rigorous; they would be woken at 0600, have breakfast and then a parade. They would then attend classes until 1600. The men were expected to remain in their barrack rooms studying during the evening. Weekends were generally free. It is significant to note that around 95 per cent passed successfully through this part of the training programme. It is also important to note that at this stage any rank that had been given to the men was probationary and they did not wear rank badges. They were clearly identified as cadets with a white band around their caps.

As we will see in this set of photographs, the standard uniform was the breeches and puttees, along with the maternity style jacket. They would also wear Sam Browne belts. As an officer they would be given sufficient funds to have their uniform made. It is not clear whether individuals that had been transferred from army units were entitled to a uniform allowance, if not they would have had to pay for it themselves.

The next stage would be being posted to a training squadron. Again in this album we will see that Lieutenant Richards carried out his training, which allowed him to fly over Brooklands.

At the beginning of the war the types of aircraft that they would be likely to encounter varied, but as time went on and certainly from 1917, training aircraft became fairly standardised. The first few flights for the cadets were as passengers. They would then, after becoming familiar with the aircraft, carry out dual instruction flights. This was the point at which many of the candidates began to be rejected for various reasons. The cadet would be required to carry out a series of manoeuvres after watching their instructor carry them out. There was a speaking tube that enabled the two to have rudimentary communication with one another. Sometimes the cadets, on being required to fly the aircraft by themselves for the first time, would simply freeze. Mercifully they were fairly short flights and at relatively low altitude. Whilst one unfortunate was up in the air, the rest of the cadets would watch from the ground, and an instructor would provide a caustic summary of his useless flying skills.

In order to carry out dual instruction there needed to be virtually no wind. Wind spelled disaster at the early stages of training. If wind did gust intermittently during flying days then there was a reasonably predictable expectation that several of the cadets would crash the aircraft when they tried to land. Given the weather conditions, lack of aircraft and the number of cadets to get through it could take a considerable amount of time before the cadets managed their required two to three hours of flight time. In fact two and a half hours was the ideal before flying solo. Some of the cadets barely managed two hours, other cadets, dependent on the demands and weather, might get as many as five hours before being required to carry out a solo flight. Sometimes the instructors would spring a solo flight on the cadet without warning. The cadet would land with his instructor and the instructor would calmly demand that the cadet take the aircraft round again and this time on their own. A cadet's early solo flight usually did not last any longer than around twenty minutes. Once the first solo flights had been carried out it was the job of the instructors to deal with bad habits that the cadets might have developed.

This system naturally meant that there was a high attrition rate in aircraft and, indeed, in cadets. For newcomers to aircraft the whole training process must have been a daunting experience, yet despite the demands, dangers, injuries and deaths, it was all designed to prepare them for duties on the front. Indeed most of the instructors were men who had already served on the front. For various reasons, they had been reassigned for work as instructors. Some of them were either physically or mentally unable to continue service at the front, yet their piloting skills still proved to be of value with the training squadrons. It is widely believed that one of the reasons for throwing cadets into the deep end, with solo flights so early, was the very real danger that a man now serving as an instructor and having survived six months on the front line did not want to die at the hands of an incompetent cadet.

This photograph shows an officer and two non-commissioned officers with their bicycles on the edge of an airfield. It should be borne in mind that the Royal Flying Corps uniform was khaki and that the pale blue was not introduced until the Royal Air Force became an independent branch of the British armed forces in April 1918. Even then many men who had served in the Royal Flying Corps or the Royal Naval Air Service continued to wear their old khaki uniforms until they wore out. This was particularly the case for officers who had to buy their own uniforms. They were allowed to continue to wear them, which meant that the changeover period from khaki to blue was long and drawn out. Even after April 1918 men coming into the newly formed Royal Air Force were still being issued with khaki uniforms, which were essentially the general service tunic of the British Army. Towards the end of 1918 there was still a khaki uniform, with a belted tunic, which for the first time had RAF badges on the shoulders. Most of the men hated the pale blue and it took until the middle of September 1919 for the blue/grey to be introduced, which has now become the standard up to the present day. It is also true that khaki uniform was still being issued until the mid-1920s.

This is a photograph of Lieutenant Richards, presumably with his grandparents or other elderly relatives, in their garden. Unlike the Second World War, rationing was only introduced during the First World War in February 1918. This was largely a protective measure to try to stop the development in food shortages. The First World War did see German U-boat actions but these were by no means as effective as the submarine campaign of the Second World War. When war was first declared in 1914 there was panic buying and most foods were generally available until at least the end of 1916. By 1917, however, the Germans had stepped up their submarine warfare campaign in the Atlantic. At various stages Britain only had a matter of weeks of basic foodstuffs, such as wheat and coal. The government had taken over 2.5 million acres of land for farming in 1917. Work on the land was largely carried out by members of the Women's Land Army and by conscientious objectors. Sugar was rationed in January 1918, margarine, cheese and butter were added along with meat in April.

Test firing a Lewis gun can be seen in this photograph. Note the bag slung underneath the gun to catch the bullet cartridges. The individuals are identified in the album as Thompson, Clarke, Mitchell and an unnamed machine gun corporal. It is interesting to see the Lewis gun on a tripod. Most standard gun firing practices for the British Army would have been carried out with the firer lying prone on the ground. The Lewis gun weighed 27lbs and it was a multipurpose machine gun. It was much lighter than heavier models and did not need water cooling. It had an easy to replace barrel. For ground troops the Lewis gun was normally fitted with a standard bipod but in this case it is using a tripod, which would normally have been used for the Vickers heavy machine gun. On aircraft they were often dual mounted and had double sized magazines.

A Royal Flying Corps cadet pilot is cutting a dash in his uniform, with a pair of high boots over his puttees. Wrapping the puttees needed quite a practised technique. The breeches would have to be laced at the calf, the puttees would then be rolled up and, holding the end of the puttee, it would be placed against the shin and unrolled towards the boot or top of the foot. At the boot top the puttee would be wrapped around the leg, with the first turn overlapping the top of the boot. Normally this would go round the boot twice and then the puttee would be wrapped around the leg, with each pass overlapping the previous one. When the puttee reached the top of the calf just below the knee a cotton tape would then be used to secure it in place. Essentially they were Indian style gaiters and originally designed to protect the lower leg whilst moving about in dense undergrowth or whilst riding.

Three Royal Flying Corps cadets are taking a well earned break between training sessions in this shot. This photograph was probably taken in Surrey in 1917. A typical cadet would spend ten times more flying time solo than under instruction. Slowly but surely solo flights would increase to around three quarters of an hour. They would also be encouraged to fly at higher altitudes to get the sense of the aircraft's manoeuvrability at different heights. Clearly at this stage if the cadets made a mistake the result was likely to be fatal. A lot of elementary flight training was done at times when the air was at its calmest. So this meant that the cadets would usually be woken up at 0500 hours to take advantage of calm air, as higher winds would build up during the course of the day and then die down towards the later afternoon when more flying could be carried out. It is not surprising that this type of training left the men exhausted and their nerves shot.

An unnamed building can be seen here, which has a cross marked on the left-hand side to indicate Lieutenant Richard's billet. This photograph was taken during the winter months of 1917 to 1918. In order to complete elementary flight training each of the pilots would have done between ten and twenty hours of solo flying. They would also have to have made thirty successful landings and, in addition, one of the landings would have to have been what was termed emergency conditions and not on their usual aerodrome. The vast majority of the men would have got used to flying BE2s and Avro 504s, although other aircraft were often used. They would then be posted for advanced training, where they would be encouraged to fly every day. Some of them were cross-country flights; others required them to make aerial observations, carry out navigation, practice bombing techniques or climb to an altitude in excess of 8,000ft. Clearly the aircraft that were being used for advanced training were more high powered aircraft and they would be expected to continue to fly even in snowy weather conditions.

Two Royal Flying Corps men are enjoying an excursion in a horse and trap. With the cadets flying for longer times and further distances there was certain inevitability about getting lost and having to land on strange aerodromes. They would also make a number of forced landings and find themselves having to spend the night many miles from their own billets. With advanced training for the first time they were introduced to aerial gunnery. They would be expected to be able to strip and reassemble their machine guns. To date the men would possibly only have fired as many as ten rounds on a Lewis gun. Before 1917 cadets would be expected to fire Lewis guns at targets being towed by a tow plane. After this time a camera gun was used. A lot of the gunnery practice was actually carried out on the ground, with targets whizzing around circular tracks. This would help teach the cadets that they had to fire ahead of the target in order to hit it.

A tented Royal Flying Corps camp can be seen here, in rural England. As the Royal Flying Corps increased in size and scope it was not just aircraft, instructors and other facilities that fell short of the requirements. Temporary camps like this to process new pilots and crews were common. Depending on the demands for pilots at the front the cadets could now be sent immediately to a front line squadron whilst others were luckier. They would continue their training for two to five months before being posted. This would enable them to clock up nearly 100 hours of flight time before facing the enemy in the air. The training improved as time went on and obviously it was desirable for the cadets to get experience on the precise type of aircraft that they would be flying in combat. Lucky pilots would get ten to thirty hours before being deployed.

This is another family shot of Lieutenant Richards, this time with two other individuals. It seems obvious from their features that they are the brothers of Lieutenant Richards. Men would not be allowed to wear their pilots' wings until they were officially qualified for service at the front. Some of the men, prior to being posted to a front line unit, may have only flown thirty hours of solo time. In order to be eligible for front line service the requirements were comparatively limited. They would have had to attend the School of Military Aeronautics, flown solo or dual for around twenty five hours and show that they were able to fly an aircraft in a satisfactory manner. They would have also had to have flown a sixty mile cross-country flight, landing twice *en route*. They would have to have flown at a height of 8,000ft for fifteen minutes and crucially they would then have to land within 50ft of a circular mark. Some pilots would also have had to have made two landings in the dark, using only flares. To get their wings they would have had to have passed all of these criteria and flown for five hours out of thirty on the squadron's main aircraft type and carried out fifteen tail-down landings.

Lieutenant Richards is sporting his helmet and goggles in this photograph. Towards the end of 1917 the minimum requirement for a front line pilot was increased to eighty hours. At least twenty hours of that figure would have to have been on the squadron's main aircraft. This was fine in theory, but in practice, with the number of pilots being killed or captured, this requirement was often ignored and replacements were sent as soon as there were losses. This was in line with an edict by Lord Trenchard that there be 'no empty chairs'.

Here we see a group of Royal Flying Corps pilots. The Royal Flying Corps cap badge had the RFC monogram inside a wreath of laurel leaves, with a crown on the top. The majority of these men are wearing British Army style trench coats. These can be traced back to a Burberry design from the Boer War. They were made of gabardine and designed to keep the wearer warm and well ventilated. They were not required parts of the uniform and had to be bought by the officer.

This is a photograph signed and dated November 15 1917. Uniforms such as these were advertised by Burberrys, who were based in the Haymarket in London. They also had provincial agents around Britain and also outfitters in Paris. They were marketed as being hygienic and efficient, which could protect the wearer against the wet and cold and were resistant to hard wear. The advertising stated that Burberry could provide a complete officer's kit in two to four days and went on to state that the uniforms were strong and lightweight, as well as the fact that during the course of the war their uniforms would be cleaned and re-proofed free of charge.

Laying out the silver trophies is the feature here. Note the standards encased and crossed on the left-hand side of the presentation table. A wide variety of different silver trophies and awards would be given out to pilots of training squadrons to commemorate their specific abilities and accomplishments. Some of these trophies may well be specific sport trophies, but are more likely to be related to gunnery, bombing and navigational excellence. Awards and trophies such as this were instrumental in motivating the men and maintaining their morale.

The sad remains of a two-seater aircraft can be seen here, which seems to have come to grief on landing. This is likely to be an Avro 504, which was in widespread use in the training squadrons. A number of two-seaters were used, including the DH6, the Armstrong Whitworth FK8, the RE8, the Sopwith 1.5 Strutter and the Vickers FB14.

This is a 1913 Krit K 25hp tourer. The Krit Motor Car Company was a small manufacturing outfit that was located in Detroit, Michigan between 1909 and 1916. The name is derived from Kenneth Crittenden, who originally designed the cars and provided most of the finances for the company. A careful look at the photograph will reveal the swastika emblem. The business failed in around 1916 and most of the vehicles were exported to Europe and Australia. There is an existing 1913 example in the National Automobile Museum in Reno, Nevada.

This is a severely damaged Avro 504k. In 2009, at the Old Rhinebeck Museum near New York, a replica Avro 504k was flying at a height of around 300ft when the engine stalled. It crashed into some swampy land, which made the top wings collapse and there was severe damage to the lower wings. Another replica suddenly lost power and crashed into trees in New Zealand in 2008. This was at the Vintage Aviator Fighter Collection Show. Back in the 1920s, when Avros were being disposed of, they would be lucky to raise £100 each. Nowadays replicas are changing hands for amounts in excess of £40,000.

This is another close up of a wrecked Avro 504k. Avro 504k losses continued after the end of the First World War. One came down, narrowly missing the Old Pavilion Theatre in Weymouth on August 16 1919. The Avro was in private hands and being flown by Captain Alan Storey. He had just picked up a female passenger with the intention of taking her to Bournemouth. A sudden engine explosion broke up the propeller and the aircraft came to grief in the sea, next to the pavilion. Both the pilot and passenger were rescued and the wreckage was towed into the harbour.

This is a nice photograph of the album's owner on an early motorcycle. Although it is difficult to identify this particular make and model, we know that the Royal Flying Corps used Phelon and Moore machines, as well as Sunbeams. A Sunbeam dated 1915, which belonged to 11 Squadron of the Royal Flying Corps, was auctioned by Bonham in 2008 with an estimate of between £12,000 and £15,000.

.This is a Royal Flying Corps captain. The tunic would have had brass collar badges. The embroidered rank pips would have been one for a second lieutenant and two for a lieutenant. By the time this photograph was taken there were already women in the Royal Flying Corps. There were all-female companies and the first of these companies enrolled on December 28 1917. Women had been working alongside the Royal Flying Corps from 1916; these were members of the British Legion, who operated as drivers. When the Royal Flying Corps and Royal Naval Air Service merged, women were encouraged to join the Women's Royal Air Force. Their main job was to work as home-based mechanics.

This is likely to be the Stoughton Barracks at Guildford in Surrey, which was a former militia barracks. It was originally suggested that it would be built in 1851, but it was eventually constructed from 1873 and completed in 1876. During the First World War, amongst many other things, the barracks were used as a recruiting centre. The army continued to use it as a barracks until 1983 and ten years later work began to convert the barracks into housing. The keep was converted into flats and the original officers' mess became luxury apartments. The men here are parading. Bear in mind that standard military discipline was an integral part of a cadet's training programme. This would be regardless of the fact that some of the men would have transferred from existing army units.

This photograph is a close up of the parade, showing the military band. The regiment that had the longest association with the barracks was the Queen's Royal West Surrey Regiment. It was raised in 1661. It used Stoughton as its home barracks from 1876 until 1959.

This is a photograph of a Royal Flying Corps pilot in a long leather coat. These were worn from around 1915. Due to the fact that the First World War aircraft had open cockpits they needed something significant to keep them warm at higher altitudes and at lower temperatures. It was not until 1926 that a sheepskin flying jacket was designed by a parachute engineer, Leslie Irvin. This would become the iconic flying jacket that would be used by the Royal Air Force during the Second World War.

Here we see a second shot of the pilot in the long leather coat. The Americans adapted this type of coat and produced a shorter, four-pocketed version, which was also double-breasted. It became synonymous with interwar Barnstormer pilots. It was not as bulky but it was warm and fairly waterproof. The Americans produced these shorter versions until the late-1930s. The Barnstormer was often seen being worn by stunt pilots and members of flying circuses. It was even in the Sears catalogue.

A Royal Flying Corps second lieutenant is featured here with his bicycle. The Austin Motor Company produced a number of RE7 aircraft. Unfairly it has often been described as being one of the least effective aircraft ever used. It was supposed to have a speed of 82mph but for the majority of the aircraft 60mph was a more achievable speed. It was prone to spinning out of control, it was difficult to manoeuvre and it would often stall. Some members of the Royal Flying Corps suggested that it was so bad that when it was flying on a windy day, someone pedalling furiously on a bicycle could outpace it.

This shot was probably taken during Lewis gun training, as the individual on the left was identified on another photograph as being a Lewis machine gunner. For two-seater Royal Flying Corps aircraft the main job of the observer, aside from assisting in identifying location and targets, was to man the Lewis gun. Sometimes they would have two on a ring. The men would have to be expert in being able to assemble, clean and dismantle the gun. Both men's lives would depend on the weapon. It was quite a cumbersome job to try to swing the Lewis gun around even though it was mounted on a ring. The speed of aerial combat was so rapid that this made the job of tracking targets almost impossible.

This photograph is captioned as having been taken at Weybridge Park in May 1917, and as showing the mess hall. It would appear that this was at the time Weybridge Park College. It had been a private house that had been owned by the Churchill family. After the war, between 1919 and 1926, it became a boy's school. The home at the time was owned by Fraser Churchill, who was a renowned English rower. He had actually immigrated to Australia in 1894 but he was the son of Charles Churchill and we must presume that until the end of the First World War it was still in the Churchill family.

This is the rear of Weybridge Park House in Surrey. The caption states that the photograph was taken from the main Royal Flying Corps camp site. This would make perfect sense, as Weybridge Park is close to Brooklands. Other photographs in the album show Lieutenant Richards in flight over Brooklands.

It would appear that this photograph was taken in the grounds of Weybridge Park House and this is a timber-clad outbuilding. Note that three of the men are wearing the Royal Flying Corps maternity style jackets and two are wearing standard British Army style jackets. One of the men is wearing a Royal Flying Corps side cap. It had bronze buttons and a Royal Flying Corps cap badge.

Richards is in his British Army style Royal Flying Corps officer's jacket here, sporting lieutenants' pips on the cuff. Many of the officers in the Royal Flying Corps had a tendency to wear the insignia of the unit from which they had originally been attached. This was instead of wearing standard Royal Flying Corps insignia. As in this case, the officer is wearing his standard Army service dress. It was more of a tendency for non-commissioned officers and other ranks to wear the maternity jacket. The maternity jacket, although an odd shape, was actually quite practical and it was designed specifically for flying duties. It had concealed buttons, which were an advantage.

Richards' billet is featured here, with an improvised plotting table. Note the measuring tools. This would presumably have allowed him to practice his navigational lessons.

A captain is in his Army service dress, with swagger stick and leather gloves. Judging by the buildings in the background this photograph was probably taken at Stoughton barracks. Undoubtedly this photograph was taken prior to a parade. Note the colour difference between the jacket and the breeches and that the officer is wearing high boots rather than short boots and puttees.

Several of the Royal Flying Corps pilots are in their Army service dress here. All are wearing the British Army style jacket, breeches, short boots and puttees. Many of the Royal Flying Corps officers' peak caps were actually made in India. One notable manufacturer was Ramji Dass and Co. They were based in the city of Sialkot, which is now part of Pakistan. The cap was made from green wool and was essentially a visor hat.

This photograph was taken at Bangor and it shows Richards on the left, a lieutenant called Constable in the centre and a third individual, Snelgrove, on the right. The airfield at Bangor in Wales opened in July 1918. The only buildings that still remain on the site are now part of a farm and it would appear that very little of the airfield is still in existence. However, judging by the background, this is in fact Bangor in County Down, which would make sense as Richards was certainly in Belfast and Londonderry for a period of time whilst he was under training with the Royal Flying Corps. The assumption must be that this photograph was taken during a short period of leave.

This is the first of a group of five photographs that show the terrible damage done by a relatively weak storm to a number of aircraft. The aircraft are FE2Bs. In this first photograph we can see the D8060. This aircraft came into production towards the end of 1915 and was deployed as a front line fighter in January 1916. It was a pilot flying an FE2B that killed the German ace Max Immelmann on June 18 1916.

Here we can see two more serial numbers; D9077 and D907? Note in the foreground that we can see the remains of the frame of the canvas-built hangar that had stored these aircraft.

Several numerals are visible in this photograph; D9077, D697?, D8080 and others in the jumbled mess. It seems that some of the aircraft suffered considerably more damage by being tipped over, whilst others appear to have suffered relatively little visible damage. The FE2B was a two-seater and was 9.83m long. It had a wingspan of 14.55m and the observer would be armed with a Lewis gun, which would either be a single weapon or mounted as a pair.

It is just possible to see on the fuselage of one of these aircraft the name Grahame White. The Grahame White Aviation Company was founded by Claude Grahame White. He was the first man to make a night flight in a race from London to Manchester in 1910, sponsored by the *Daily Mail*. His company manufactured aircraft for the Royal Flying Corps during the course of the war. He had established his company at Hendon in 1911. He made several of his own types of aircraft, including his Type XV, which was known as the 'Box Kite' and was a military trainer. Grahame White's company ceased operations in 1924. In the post-war years they went on to make cars.

The Royal Air Force Museum in Hendon has an FE2B. By April 1918 seven squadrons were using the FE2D for night bombing missions. They were also being used for night flying training. The FE2B was unique in many respects, but principally it was its simple design that allowed factories with limited experience in building aircraft to make it. In many respects it was one of the very first large production aircraft designs.

This crumpled aircraft only reveals C97 as part of its serial number. Again this would imply this is almost certainly a Bristol F2B. This was a two-seater biplane fighter that was agile, solidly designed and affectionately nicknamed Biff. It was designed by Frank Barnwell and it first flew in September 1916. Over 5,300 of these aircraft were built and at 1919 prices the cost of the aircraft was £1,350.

This wreck only reveals a B and is extremely difficult therefore to identify. To put aircraft losses into perspective, when war broke out in August 1914 the British only had 113 aircraft in service. Just over a year later they had twelve squadrons and a total of 161 aircraft. By July 1916 this had risen to twenty seven squadrons with over 600 aircraft. However, in the second battle of the Somme, which was triggered off by a German offensive in March 1918, the Royal Flying Corps lost 1,000 aircraft in one month. Many of these were lost as a result of the Germans, shelling of airfields. Losses continued and in August 1918 some 100 aircraft were lost on August 8 alone. This was out of nearly 850 for the month. The Royal Air Force, as it now was, by the armistice in November 1918 had 1,782 front line aircraft.

This is the first of a series of fascinating photographs of Lieutenant Richards in the role of a cadet observer over Brooklands Racecourse, at a height of 5,000ft, sometime in 1917. The photograph was taken by the pilot.

This again is some 5,000ft over Brooklands. The photograph has had a double exposure and, as Richards describes it, it is a skeleton photograph of Lieutenant Pollack, whom he identifies as being the pilot of the aircraft. Below is Virginia Water, which is a stretch of water near Old Windsor and Ascot and close to Windsor Great Park.

Richards identifies this as being Brooklands track from the air. Brooklands was opened in 1907. It was a purpose-built motor sport venue, but also one of the very first airfields. By 1918 huge numbers of aircraft were being built on the site. Vickers Aviation had set up a factory there in 1915. It was extensively used to test and build military aircraft.

This photograph would have been taken very early in Richards' Royal Flying Corps career, as the insignia on the cuff suggests that he was a second lieutenant at the time. The uniform is probably khaki and he is not wearing breeches but standard issue British Army trousers. It was the Royal Flying Corps that coined the phrase 'flying officer'. When the RAF was created officer ranks were taken from the British Army but when the RAF created their own rank structure in August 1919 lieutenants became flying officers. This dates back to the First World War period, which simply denoted that the individual had flying duties and it was not a rank as such.

This is a Crossley truck, or more accurately a tender. The Royal Air Force Museum has a light tender. The first of these were delivered to the Royal Flying Corps in 1913. By the end of the First World War there were around 6,000 of them in service. By the mid-1920s over 300 were still in service and many of these were being used abroad.

This is the billet being used by Richards at Croydon in May 1917. At Croydon there was an airfield at Beddington, which had been established in May 1915, primarily for use by Home Defence squadrons against the Zeppelins. There was another airfield opened at Waddon in 1918, next door to an aircraft factory. Croydon airport itself did not actually officially open until March 1920. It was made up of the two original airfields, separated by a road.

This photograph is captioned as having been taken at the Eastern Command School in Bedford in 1917. The man with a pipe second from the left is the original owner of the album. The two men either side of him are respectively named as Potter and Scott. Eastern Command was established in 1905. Although its headquarters was at Horse Guards, it used several sites around the Bedford area, including Kempstone Barracks, Russell Park and Biscot. Eastern Command was much like the other British Army home commands, such as London, District, Northern, Scottish, Southern, Western, Channel Islands, Irish and Aldershot. It had a mix of different units ranging from the Army Service Corps, Veterinary Corps, Royal Engineers and the Royal Flying Corps. It also had attached artillery and was directly responsible when war broke out in 1914 for the British 4th Division.

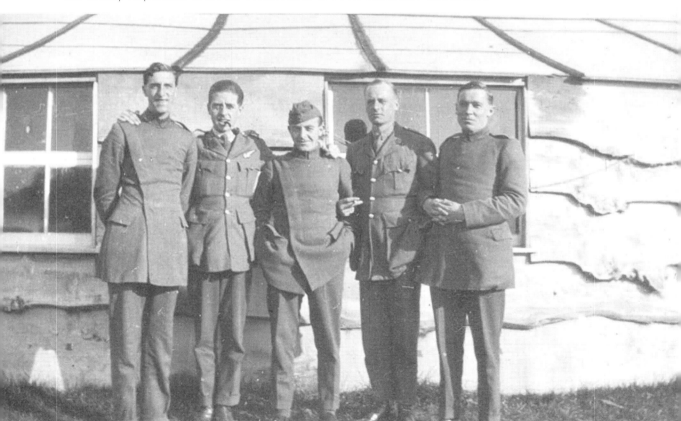

This photograph shows the album owner's room at Deanfield in Londonderry. This may well be part of the larger Ebrington Barracks complex. Ebrington Barracks has a long association with the British Army and it was first used during the siege of Derry between 1688 and 1689. A fort was built there, with the canon batteries pointing towards Derry. A new star fort was built on the site in 1841 and it was further expanded in 1875. During the First World War it was used as a temporary base by several different regiments. The site is now an arts centre and the former parade ground an open air performance space.

This is labelled as showing an officers' mess in Belfast. Interestingly enough the motto of the Royal Flying Corps and later the Royal Air Force can be linked directly to an officers' mess. The first commanding officer of the Royal Flying Corps was Colonel Frederick Sykes. He asked his men to try and come up with a motto that would be suitable for this new organisation. Two junior officers were leaving the officers' mess at Farnborough and apparently one of them, J S Yule, came up with the phrase *per ardua ad astra*. It was based on a phrase from the Roman poet Virgil. Sykes liked the idea and so too did King George V and it was approved. Yule had seen the phrase in a book written by Rider Haggard, where he had described the motto as being on a coat of arms. Haggard probably got it from the Mulway family in Ireland, who had used it as their family motto for several generations.

This photograph is captioned as having been taken at Staines in 1917. Although this is a photograph of Richards and he identifies it as having been taken at Staines, it is more than likely that this was almost certainly Hounslow Heath, which was also known as RFC Hounslow. It was probably opened in 1910 and remained open until March 1920. Currently it is disused open land. It had previously been a British Army cavalry barracks and the first aircraft had landed there in 1909, with a hangar being constructed in the following year.

This is another photograph of Richards standing by his aircraft in a hangar at Hounslow Heath in May 1917. In 1917 we know that No 85 Squadron, commanded by Billy Bishop, later an Air Marshal, was stationed at Hounslow Heath. They flew SE5As. By December 87 Squadron spent time there, again with SE5As. Prior to that 52 Squadron was based at Hounslow Heath. They were a reconnaissance squadron.

This would appear to be the same building, probably in Croydon, as we can see Richards' motorcycle in the background. Richards captions this photograph as showing three of his fellow pilots. He also notes that all of these men were killed in air combat over France.

This is another shot of Richards with the 1913 Krit K 25hp tourer. Richards has captioned this photograph as featuring 'the tank'. The vehicle was advertised as having a streamlined, graceful body with a tapered bonnet, electric lights and an electric starter if the purchaser required. In the United States the vehicle sold for $950 or an extra $100 if it had an electric starter. It boasted that the transmission gears were made from chrome nickel steel and that they were case hardened.

The final photograph in this album features Captain H E Cherry. It has not been possible to trace this individual but what is known is that the photograph was taken in Weybridge, probably in 1917. As to whether or not Captain Cherry went on to become a Royal Flying Corps pilot or not is unknown.

Chapter 4

Seaplanes on the River Crouch

Although the focus of these photographs is a series of shots of a short seaplane Type 184 on the River Crouch, they are in fact part of a much larger album that belonged to a Lieutenant William John Shorter.

Shorter was unfortunately killed in action on March 23 1918. He had been born in Birmingham around 1898. He was only twenty years old at the time of his death. Official records reveal some slight confusion about his previous military experience. On the one hand he is shown as having been seconded to the Royal Air Force in January 1918 from the Essex Regiment Territorial. An alternative card from the index states that he came from the 8th (Cyclist Battalion) Territorial. Both of these, however, are related to the 8th Territorial Battalion connected to the Essex Regiment.

At the time of Shorter's death he was attached to Royal Flying Corps Squadron No 46. His Sopwith Camel had the serial number B9195. No 46 Squadron was based at Filescamp Farm near Arras in France. They were engaged in low level ground attacks on German positions in order to counter a new German offensive that had been launched in the Picardy region on March 21 1918. Only a day or so before his death Shorter, flying a Sopwith Camel serial number C1613, was forced to land prematurely after having taken severe damage from ground fire.

There is actual confusion over the nature of Shorter's death. On one card he is simply stated as having been killed in action, whilst the other suggests that there was an accident that led to his death.

Shorter's squadron, No 46, was originally part of No 2 Reserve Squadron, which had been based at Wyton, near St Ives in Cambridgeshire. They made the move to France in April 1916 and for the next year they were primarily involved in reconnaissance work. In May 1917 their Nieuport aircraft were replaced with Sopwith Pups. In the July they were shifted to Sutton's Farm in Essex to help protect London from Gotha bomber attacks. They were back in France by August, however, and were involved in the attack that became known as the battle of Messines.

The squadron was issued with Sopwith Camels in November 1917. One of the most successful pilots of the squadron also joined the unit that month. Donald MacLaren, a Canadian, and an individual instrumental in creating the Royal Canadian Air Force, began to clock up enemy kills. By the end of the war he had fifty four. This consisted of six balloons and forty eight aircraft.

Victor Yeates, who went on to write *Winged Victory*, also joined the squadron in 1918. By the end of the war 46 Squadron had at least sixteen aces and they had accounted for eighty four enemy aircraft and balloons. The squadron was deactivated at the end of 1919 but reemerged in 1936. By the beginning of the Second World War they were flying Hawker Hurricanes. The squadron was involved in the Battle of Britain, it was then sent to Malta and then to North Africa. The squadron was finally dissolved in 1975.

The first four photographs in this small collection feature the variously named Short Admiralty Type 184 or the Short 225. It was designed to be a reconnaissance aircraft and a torpedo bomber. It had folded wings and made its first flight in 1915 and remained in service until 1918. The aircraft has the distinction of being the very first aircraft to ever sink a ship using a torpedo. Short seaplanes were also the only aircraft to be used during the battle of Jutland.

These photographs were taken on the River Crouch. For many years an airfield on the Isle of Sheppey was believed to be the oldest aerodrome in Britain. Although these photographs do not feature Fambridge but the river itself, the Fambridge location is now gradually being recognised as having played a key role in the development of aircraft. Many pioneers visited the site, particularly before the First World War. There was an aircraft factory at Fambridge prior to 1909. It was a short-lived existence, but there was certainly aviation experiments carried out on the River Crouch around 1914. We know that the flying boat, the *Talbot Quick*, was tested there. The reason for the association with flying boats was to make use of the shipbuilding expertise in the area.

The tests that were carried out in 1914 obviously proved the point that this part of the River Crouch was ideal for testing seaplanes. In the Fambridge area the river is both wide and straight. In fact it is around 300m wide and it is relatively deep at high tide, being virtually straight for over 4km.

Unfortunately we are not able to identify exactly when these photographs were taken. Much of the trials, including the torpedo dropping, took place in 1914. By March 1915 two of the prototypes were actually sent to play a role in the Gallipoli campaign.

It was on August 12 1915 that a crippled enemy ship was attacked by a Short Type 184 being piloted by Charles Humphrey Kingsman Edmonds, who would later become an Air Vice Marshal. The target, a Turkish merchant ship, was attacked by Edmonds and he hit it. A full victory, giving both Edmonds and the aircraft immortality, occurred on August 17, when a second Turkish vessel was sunk for the first time using an aerial torpedo attack.

Here we can see the two-seater Short seaplane Type 184 slowly making its way along the River Crouch. It is probably taxiing before takeoff and trying to avoid the obvious obstacles of the moored vessels. The aircraft was designed by Horace Short. The fuselage was essentially a braced wooden box and the wings could be swung out using a hand winch in the cockpit. There were two main floats and a third wooden tail float, with a small water rudder. The crew were able to communicate with a radio transmitter and a receiver. This was powered using a wind-driven generator. If this failed a basket of carrier pigeons was carried as a precaution. Initially, ten aircraft were ordered, but subsequently at least ten manufacturers built another 936. The aircraft became very useful in an anti-submarine role. There is no record, however, that the aircraft ever managed to sink an enemy submarine. By December 1918 over 300 of these seaplanes were still in service and some would remain in use until around 1920. They were officially taken off the equipment lists by around 1922.

This is a second shot of the Short seaplane Type 184. This has now been moored in shallow water and we can see what appears to be a Royal Naval launch in the background. It is also just possible to make out the serial number of the seaplane, 3068. The serial number is a little confusing, as the Royal Navy assigned 2900 to 2999 for the Short Type 184. They had previously assigned 2790 to 2849 and 2600 to 2659 to this particular type of aircraft. There was also 1080 to 1099, 1130 to 1149, 1220 to 1279, 1580 to 1624, 1630 to 1689, 1740 to 1774, 1780 to 1799, 1820 to 1839, and, later, 9000 to 9199 and 9260 to 9449. The mystery, however, is solved when the serial number is actually compared to the Air Committee Joint Numbering System. This aircraft is part of a series of numbers allocated to the Short Admiralty Type 827 (3063 to 3072). This means that the aircraft, although a Short, was only one of around 108 aircraft ever built. This makes the aircraft, and therefore the photograph, even rarer. It shared many of the characteristics of the Short Type 184. The first flight of this aircraft was in 1914 and it had a Sunbeam Nubian engine and a two-bladed propeller. Both the Short Type 827 and the Short Type 184 are very much interrelated. The development of the Type 827 saw it being delivered to the Royal Naval Air Service in 1914. It was a direct descendent of the Short Type 166, which was also a torpedo carrying, folding seaplane.

This is a clearer shot of the layout of the aircraft, which is now being winched out of the River Crouch. It is clear to see that the personnel are almost certainly Royal Navy. The Type 827 had two crewmen; a pilot and an observer. For close protection it had a Lewis gun, which was on a mount in the rear cockpit. The overall length of the aircraft was 10.74m. It had a wingspan of 16.4 and a height of 4.11m. The Sunbeam Nubian engine was rated at 150hp. The aircraft could achieve a maximum speed of around 62mph and carried sufficient fuel onboard for a three and a half hour flight. The aircraft may well have been manufactured fairly locally, as there was a production facility at Rochester in Kent. Royal Naval air stations began to receive Type 827s around the summer of 1915. They were sent to Great Yarmouth, Grain, Calshot, Dundee and Killingholme. Type 827s were used against the German High Seas Fleet in April 1916 when they shelled Southwold and Lowestoft. Some Short Type 827s were shipped even further afield; three of them were used as spotter aircraft in East Africa. These aircraft went on to Mesopotamia, where they saw action against the Ottoman Turks in December 1915. The most travelled of the Short Type 827s were those that were flown by Belgians. Serial numbers 8219, 3093, 3094 and 3095 were flown out to Africa and transported, dismantled, to Lake Tongwe in the former Eastern Congo (now Tanzania). They were then assembled and in July 1916 they bombed the German cruiser *Graf von Goetzen*, which was lying in the port of Kigoma on Lake Tanganyika. This bombing raid directly led to the surrender of the port a few days later.

This final photograph on the River Crouch is a closer shot of the Type 827. We can see the observer in the rear cockpit and there is a clear view of the serial number on the fuselage. This Short Type 827 was certainly manufactured by the Short brothers themselves. They manufactured these Short 827 aircraft within this serial number range. Many other Short aircraft were in fact manufactured by other contractors. Westland Aircraft Works at Yeovil in Somerset produced Short 166s and Short 184s. The Brush Electrical Engineering Company Limited of Loughborough did produce a number of Short Type 827s. Aircraft with the serial numbers 3321 to 3332 and 8230 to 8335 were all made by them. they also made a significant number of Short Type 184s . Also a number of Type 827s were made by Parnall and Sons Limited in Eastville, Bristol (8218 to 8229). More 827s were made by Fairey Aviation Company Limited of Hayes, Middlesex (8550 to 8561). The Sunbeam Motorcar Company of Wolverhampton also produced Short 827s (8630 to 8649) and they also made some Short 320s. S E Saunders Ltd of East Cowes on the Isle of Wight made Short 184s, as did Mann, Egerton and Co Ltd based on the Prince of Wales Road in Norwich. More 184s were made by the Phoenix Dynamo Manufacturing Company Limited of Bradford, Frederick Sage and Company Limited of Peterborough, Robey and Co Ltd of Lincoln, J Samuel White and Co Ltd of Cowes on the Isle of Wight and the Supermarine Aviation Works Limited of Woolston, Southampton.

This is the first of two photographs that are captioned indicating that the shot was taken at Stow Maries, of a BE2E starting up to intercept German aircraft in 1917. The aircraft's serial number is clearly visible; it is A2767, which positively identifies it as a BE2E. This particular aircraft was with the Home Defence Squadron No 37, based at Goldhanger in the spring of 1917. It was then with the 2nd Wireless School at Penhurst from the winter of 1917 to the spring of 1918 before it was assigned to No 61 Squadron based at Rochford in 1918. No 37 Squadron was originally created out of a unit at the experimental station at Orford Ness in April 1916. The unit was absorbed in May, but reformed in September 1916. Its primary role was home defence to cover the southeast of England. The headquarters was at Woodham Manor, but elements of the squadron operated out of Goldhanger, Rochford and Stow Maries. One of their BE12s brought down the L48 Zeppelin over the Suffolk countryside in mid-June 1917. After the war ended the squadron was shifted to Biggin Hill in the spring of 1919. It was effectively disbanded in the July when it was renumbered as No 39 Squadron. One of the famous pilots of No 37 Squadron was Frederick Sowrey. He was born in Gloucestershire in 1893 and was a former second lieutenant in the Royal Fusiliers. After being wounded in 1915 he joined the Royal Flying Corps. Initially he was posted to No 39 Squadron in June 1916, after having undergone his flight training. Flying a BE2C he had taken off shortly before midnight on September 23 1916. Just after 0100hours he spotted the L32 Zeppelin at an altitude of around 13,000ft. Sowrey pumped three drums of incendiary ammunition into the Zeppelin and it exploded, leaving no survivors. The wreckage came down at Billericay in Essex. Sowrey was awarded the Distinguished Service Order. Towards the end of 1916 he not only became a flight commander, but was also transferred to No 37 Home Defence Squadron. He remained with this unit until the summer of 1917.

This is a photograph of the same aircraft, this time having its prop swung at Stow Maries in 1917. The airfield at Stow Maries was developed in order to counter the dual threat of Gotha bombers and Zeppelins. No 37 Home Defence Squadron was the first unit to arrive at the airfield in September 1916. A Flight was stationed at Rochford and there was another flight at Gardener's Farm at Goldhanger. The squadron was responsible for the eastern aerial defence of London. To begin with Stow Maries simply consisted of some basic wooden huts and tents. The first station commander was only twenty years old, but he was already a Royal Flying Corps veteran. He was Lieutenant Claude Ridley. No 37 Squadron trained and prepared at Stow Maries and Ridley, who had now become a captain, along with Lieutenant Keddie, took off on the night of May 23 to 24 1917 to intercept Zeppelins making for London. This was Stow Maries first operational mission. The flight that was assigned to Goldhanger scored the first kill for the squadron on June 17 1917. Lieutenant L P Watkins is credited with having destroyed the L48 Zeppelin over Theberton in Suffolk. This is a notable victory for No 37 Squadron, as it was the last Zeppelin ever to be shot down over Britain during the First World War. The squadron faced a considerable task on July 7 1917. They were ordered to intercept over twenty Gotha bombers that were making for London. The Rochford flight was shifted to Stow Maries that summer and Ridley left to create a new squadron that was forming at Rochford. The BE2E came into service with the Royal Flying Corps in 1912. The BE stands for Blériot Experimental and the aircraft was not an unqualified success. Around 3,500 of them were built. They were primarily reconnaissance aircraft but they were also used in a light bomber role and as night fighters. As the First World War continued it became abundantly clear that the BE2 was obsolete and it was reduced to the role of a communications aircraft, as a trainer and it was also used against submarines. It was a vulnerable aircraft and the BE2C version was nicknamed Fokker Fodder by British newspapers. The Germans simply called it Cold Meat. The BE2E seen in this photograph was the final version of the aircraft. It had new wings and was supposed to be much better than the BE2C. Its nickname was Quirk but it was really no better than its predecessor.